22802

J 551.5
Boc

Bocknek, Jonathan
The science of the sky

DATE DUE

MEDIALOG INC
ALEXANDRIA KY 41001

D1318532

The Science of the Sky

LIVING SCIENCE

Jonathan Bocknek

Gareth Stevens Publishing
MILWAUKEE

For a free color catalog describing Gareth Stevens' list of high-quality books and multimedia programs, call 1-800-542-2595 (USA) or 1-800-461-9120 (Canada). Gareth Stevens Publishing's Fax: (414) 225-0377.

Library of Congress Cataloging-in-Publication Data available upon request from publisher. Fax (414) 225-0377 for the attention of the Publishing Records Department.

ISBN 0-8368-2574-8 (lib. bdg.)

This edition first published in 2000 by
Gareth Stevens Publishing
1555 North RiverCenter Drive, Suite 201
Milwaukee, WI 53212 USA

Project Co-ordinator: Meaghan Craven
Series Editor: Linda Weigl
Copy Editors: Kristen Higgins and Heather Kissock
Design and Illustration: Warren Clark and Chantelle Sales
Cover Design: Carole Knox
Layout: Lucinda Cage
Gareth Stevens Editor: Patricia Lantier-Sampon

Every reasonable effort has been made to trace ownership and to obtain permission to reprint copyright material. The publishers would be pleased to have any errors or omissions brought to their attention so that they may be corrected in subsequent printings.

Photograph Credits:
Corel Corporation: cover (background), pages 4, 5 right, 7, 8 right, 9 right, 10, 11 bottom, 12, 13 left, 14 bottom, 17, 24 top, 30 top, 31 bottom; CU Nim Gliding Club: page 14; Digital Vision Ltd.: cover (center)pages 6, 20, 25, 26, 30 bottom, 31 center; NASA: pages 15, 28; Tom Stack & Associates: pages 13 right, 18 far left, 18 far right, 19, 27 top, 31 top; JD Taylor: 8 left, 9 left; Visuals Unlimited: pages 5 left, 11 top (Steve McCutcheon), 16, 18 left, 18 right, 22 (Jay Pasachoff), 24 bottom (David Matherly), 27 center, 27 bottom (Mark E. Gibson), 29.

Printed in Canada

1 2 3 4 5 6 7 8 9 04 03 02 01 00

Contents

What Do You Know about the Sky?

Imagine looking at the sky for the first time. You see the rich blue color, the white clouds, and the bright yellow Sun. Birds swoop from tree to tree. A storm approaches. You watch as bolts of bright light crackle across the sky. When the storm blows away, a colorful rainbow appears.

One of the best ways to explore the sky on a clear day is in a small airplane.

As day becomes night, the Moon rises slowly. Stars wink and blink at you from their places deep in space. If you live in the north, you might see a curtain of light called the **northern lights**.

Near or far, day or night, there are always things to see and wonder about in the sky.

Activity

Eye Spy
How many sky objects can you name in one minute? Time yourself with a friend or family member.

The Moon is the closest body to Earth. It is 235,000 miles (380,000 kilometers) away.

The best places to see the beautiful colors of the northern lights are in the northern areas of countries like Canada, Norway, and Russia.

The Sun

O ur most familiar daytime sky object is the Sun. The Sun is a huge ball of swirling gases. It is so big that one million planets the size of Earth could fit inside, and there would still be room for more.

The Sun is 93 million miles (150 million kilometers) away from us. A space shuttle would take about eight months to travel that far. It takes about eight minutes for the Sun's heat and light to reach Earth.

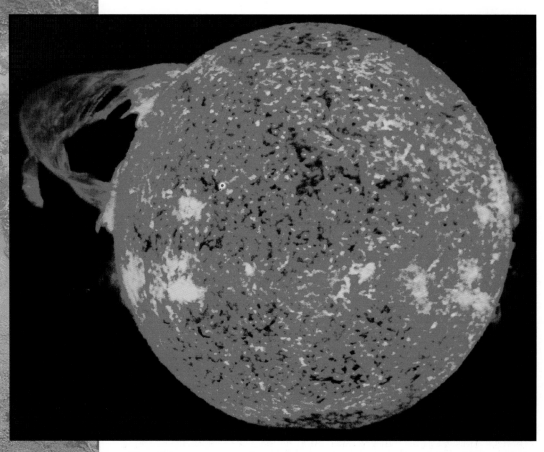

Solar flares occur when the Sun's gases react with each other. These gases create temperatures hot enough to melt iron.

Does eight minutes seem like a long time? For us and all living things, it is just the right amount of time. If the heat came faster, it would be too hot. If the heat came slower, it would be too cold. We depend on the Sun for heat and light.

All green plants use the Sun's energy to make food.

Animal life relies on the Sun for warmth. Lizards cannot keep warm without the Sun.

Puzzler

True or False?

1. The Sun always rises in the east.
2. On very hot days, you can fry an egg on the sidewalk.

Answers:
1. True, with two exceptions. When it is summer at the North Pole, the Sun does not set. When it is winter, the Sun does not rise. The same is true at the South Pole.
2. True. The Sun's heat can warm up pavement so much that it becomes hot enough to fry an egg. Try it!

Clouds

The air around us always has **water vapor** in it. We cannot see water vapor because it is an invisible gas. Water vapor is the moisture that we feel in the air. When water vapor rises in the sky, it cools and changes into tiny droplets of water. These droplets form clouds.

There are four main types of clouds. They received their names because of their shape.

Types of Clouds

Cirrus - "curl"

Cumulus - "heaped"

Cirrus clouds are wispy and float very high in the sky.

Cumulus clouds look like heaps of fluffy cotton.

Clouds can help tell what the weather will be. We can tell if it will rain, snow, or be sunny by the types of clouds in the sky and how they are moving. For example, when small cumulus clouds come together and begin to grow upward in the sky, a thunderstorm may be about to start.

Activity

Make a Cloud Map

Many people like to find shapes like bunny ears or heads in clouds. Do you? Take a piece of paper and a pencil outdoors and lie down on the grass. Watch the clouds move overhead. What kinds of shapes do you see? Make a cloud map and label the shapes you see.

Stratus - "layered"

Nimbus - "halo"

Stratus clouds look like white sheets. When they are close to the ground, we call them fog.

Nimbus clouds are dark gray rain clouds. In the winter, they bring snow.

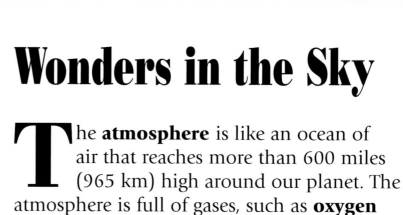

Wonders in the Sky

The **atmosphere** is like an ocean of air that reaches more than 600 miles (965 km) high around our planet. The atmosphere is full of gases, such as **oxygen** and water vapor.

Sunlight sometimes bends in the atmosphere and makes a halo around the Sun. When this happens, **sundogs** may appear on either side of the Sun.

When sunlight meets the gases in the atmosphere, it creates beautiful sights. Sometimes sunlight bounces off gases and ice crystals. Sometimes it bends as it passes through them. Rainbows and sundogs appear because of this bending and bouncing of light.

When water vapor from an airplane freezes, it forms tiny ice crystals. These crystals trail behind the airplane and look like smoke.

A rainbow is an arc of colors that appears in the sky. Rainbows form when light bends around water droplets.

Activity

Make a Rainbow

On the next sunny day, make your own rainbow. You will need a watering can or a garden hose that makes a fine mist.

1. Stand so the Sun is behind you.
2. Turn on the water and spray a fine mist of tiny water droplets in front of you. If you do not have a hose, you can use a watering can.
3. Do you see bands of color? Can you make them move? Does it matter if you spray the water higher or lower? Try making rainbows in different ways.

Floating in the Sky

Have you ever heard people describe something as being lighter than air? Very few things are lighter than air. Hot air balloons can float because the air inside them is warmer than the air outside. Hot air is lighter than cool air. As long as the air inside the balloon stays warm, the balloon will float. When the air inside the balloon cools, the balloon will come down.

Pilots control a balloon by heating or cooling the air inside the balloon.

A blimp is filled with gases that are lighter than air.

Other balloons float because they are filled with gases that are lighter than air. **Hydrogen** is one of these gases. **Helium** is the other. These gases are the two most common gases in the universe. Our Sun and all the stars in the night sky are made up mainly of hydrogen and helium.

Weather balloons can be filled with hydrogen or helium. These balloons have equipment that helps scientists predict the weather.

Puzzler

Some objects can float in the sky for a long time. Other objects stay in the sky for very short periods of time. How many examples of floating objects can you think of?

Answer:
Maybe you thought of dandelion fluff when it floats on the wind. The seeds of maple trees twirl through the air like tiny helicopters. Soap bubbles float around for a short while, until they burst. Kites float in the air, too.

Flying High

An airplane is as heavy as three hundred cars or more. How can it lift off the ground and stay in the sky? The answer involves four forces: thrust, drag, lift, and gravity.

Thrust is a **force** that pushes an airplane forward. Drag is a force that pulls an airplane backward. These forces help airplanes go fast and slow.

A glider plane does not have a motor. It relies on wind to keep it in the air.

Airplanes and jets are designed to be sleek and trim. This helps decrease the drag force.

Lift is the force that pushes an airplane up. Gravity is a force that pulls an airplane down and keeps it on the ground. These forces help airplanes go up and down.

Space shuttles, such as the Discovery, must be pushed out of the atmosphere with rockets.

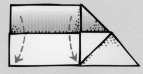

Activity

Make a Paper Airplane

You can find instructions for making paper airplanes in many books. Here is a very simple paper airplane to get you started.

1. Take a sheet of paper.
2. Fold it down the middle length-wise.
3. Open the fold. Fold the corners of one end of the paper to meet the fold in the middle. They should look like two triangles with their sides touching.

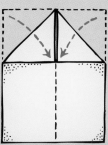

4. Fold down the middle again. Then fold the long edges so that each edge touches the folded edge, one on each side.
5. Hold the airplane along the fold and point its nose upward and outward. Move your arm back and then forward, letting the airplane glide away. How far does your airplane glide?

The Sky's the Limit

Meteorologists are scientists who want to understand the sky. They are fascinated by the Sun, the clouds, and the weather. Meteorologists study the sky and its effects. They can tell us what they think the weather will be like in the future.

Some meteorologists work outside, collecting information about the weather.

There are many other jobs involving the sky. Pilots and astronauts spend much of their time in the sky flying aircraft. Forest firefighters drop from the sky in parachutes to fight fires. Some scientists, such as astronomers, study the stars and planets.

Aerobatic pilots often perform tricks to entertain crowds at air shows.

Activity

Do Your Own Research
Find out if you are interested in these sky-related careers:

- aerobatic pilot
- air traffic controller
- airline attendant
- atmospheric scientist
- astronaut
- astronomer
- pilot

Astronauts must understand science and math to do their job. They often train for many years before they go on a mission.

The Moon and Its Phases

The Moon is our most familiar night sky object. When it is full, it looks like a bright circle in the sky. The Moon does not make its own light. It **reflects** light from the Sun.

Moon Phases

New Moon	Crescent Moon	Half Moon	Full Moon
A new moon occurs when the Moon is between the Sun and Earth. The side of the Moon facing Earth receives no sunshine and looks dark.	A crescent moon appears as the Moon **orbits** Earth. The crescent grows as more and more sunlight reaches the Earth side of the Moon.	A half moon appears when the Sun shines on half of the Earth side of the Moon.	A full moon occurs when the Sun shines on all of the Earth side of the Moon.

Approximate Time Schedule

Day 1	Day 3	Day 8	Day 15

The Moon is always changing. One night, it may be a circle. A week later, it may look cut in half. A week after that, you may not see it at all. Then, the Moon will slowly reappear. These changes in the Moon are called the phases of the Moon. It takes about one month for all the phases of the Moon to occur.

Activity

Make the Moon's Phases

1. Find a room that is lit only by one lamp.
2. Ask a friend to hold a ball in front of the lamp. Pretend the ball is the moon.

3. Stand behind your friend and face the light. Does the ball look dark? This is what it looks like when there is a new moon.
4. Stand in different places around the ball. When does it look like a half moon? When does it look like a crescent moon?

Half Moon	Crescent Moon	New Moon
A half moon appears again as the Moon continues its orbit around Earth.	The half moon turns back into a crescent moon as the Moon nears the end of its orbit.	Another new moon occurs when the Moon has completed its orbit around Earth.

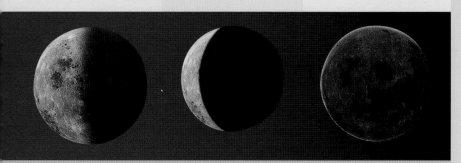

Day 22	Day 25	Day 29

The Planets

The brightest stars in the night sky are not stars at all. They are planets. There are nine planets in our **Solar System**. Five planets are visible to the human eye. These planets are Mercury, Venus, Mars, Jupiter, and Saturn. We need binoculars or a **telescope** to see two other planets – Uranus and Neptune. Pluto is too far away to be seen from Earth.

Except for Pluto, all the planets in our solar system are visible with small telescopes or our own eyes.

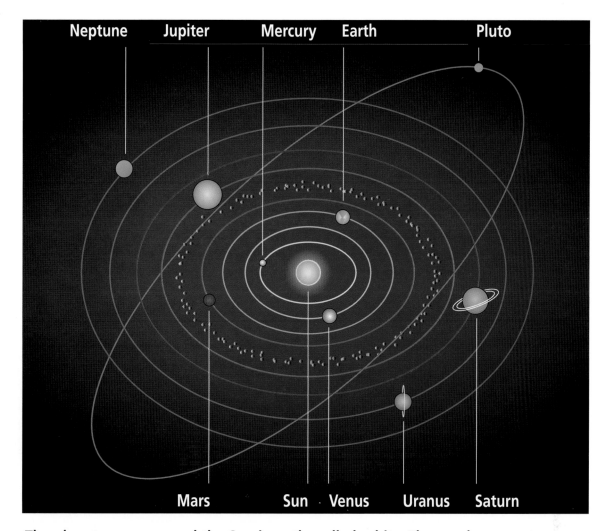

Neptune   Jupiter   Mercury   Earth   Pluto

Mars   Sun · Venus   Uranus   Saturn

The planets move around the Sun in paths called orbits. They each move at different speeds because each one is a different size and distance from the Sun.

Puzzler

Long ago, people called Venus both the Morning Star and the Evening Star. Why do you think they did this?

Answer:
Venus is visible in the evening as well as in the morning. Since Venus looks like a very bright star, people called it the Morning Star and the Evening Star. This was before anyone knew that Venus is really a planet.

Star Patterns

On a clear, dark night, you can see many stars in the sky. Some of these stars are dazzlingly bright. Others are very dim. The nearest star is named Alpha Centauri. It is very far away from Earth. A space shuttle traveling at its fastest speed would take about seventy thousand years to reach this star. Most stars are much, much farther away from us than Alpha Centauri.

There are over 200 billion stars in the universe. Most of them are so far away we cannot see them in the sky.

Long ago, people saw shapes in the stars. Some of the shapes were animals like a goat and a bear. Others were shapes of people from old tales and legends. We call these shapes in the stars constellations.

If you watched the stars all night long, you would see them move across the sky. Only one star would stay in the same place the entire night. This star is known as the North Star because it sits above the North Pole. People have used it to help them find north and other directions for thousands of years.

The North Star is in the constellation Ursa Minor, or Little Bear. Ursa Major, or Big Bear, is right below it. Some people call these constellations the big and little dippers.

Activity

Make Your Own Constellations

1. Use a sharp pencil to carefully poke small holes in one side of a shoebox. Plan the shape of the holes, or just poke them anywhere you want.
2. Ask an adult to help you cut out a square in the other side of the shoebox.
3. Shut off the lights.
4. Shine a flashlight through the square, and look at the shape of light dots on the wall.
5. Make up names for the constellations you have made.

Night Sky Sightings

The Moon and stars are familiar night sky objects because they are always visible. Other night sky objects, such as **meteors**, appear less often. Scientists can usually tell when a new sighting will appear because they study what happens in the sky. People are discovering new night sky sights, such as **comets**, meteors, and **nebulas**, all the time.

Meteors are pieces of rock that burn when they fall through the atmosphere. If they land on Earth, they make deep holes called craters. This crater is almost 1 mile (1.6 km) wide and 570 feet (174 meters) deep.

Nebulas are cloudy places in the night sky. A star might be forming or dying here.

Comets are huge balls of ice, rock, and frozen gases. When a comet comes near the Sun, it starts to melt. The melting parts of the comet form a fuzzy, glowing tail that extends behind it as it moves.

Puzzler

People in southern parts of the world sometimes see a sky effect that they call the southern lights. What do you think they are?

Answer:
The southern lights are just like the northern lights but at the South Pole. Like the northern lights, the southern lights happen when the Sun's high-energy particles meet the atmosphere near the pole.

Satellites

A satellite is an object that travels in an orbit around another larger object. For example, the Moon is a satellite because it orbits Earth.

For many years, the only satellites were natural ones, such as the Moon. Now, there are satellites that have been made by humans. Some satellites carry cameras to take pictures of Earth. Other satellites carry equipment that helps people talk to each other on telephones and computers.

Seven planets in our Solar System have natural satellites, or moons. Earth has one. Saturn has twenty-three.

Satellites can help people talk on the telephone and watch television.

In the early morning or evening, you may see a satellite moving through the sky. Satellites are bright like stars, but they move more quickly. The next time you are outside at night or in the early morning, look up. If you see a tiny star moving smoothly across the sky, it might be a satellite!

Some satellites take pictures of events and objects in space.

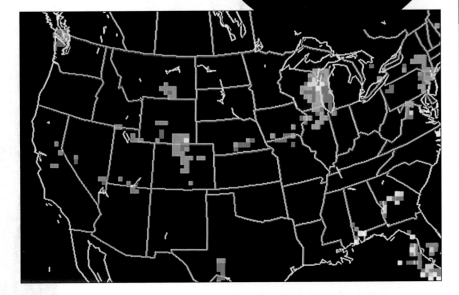

Pictures of Earth that are taken by satellites help many people. For example, they can help people predict what the weather will be.

Puzzler

How many natural satellites can you name?

Answer: All the planets except for Mercury and Venus have moons in orbit around them, so all of these moons are satellites. All the planets (and their moons) are satellites, because they all orbit the Sun. Comets that stay in orbit around the Sun are satellites, too.

Garbage in the Sky

Wherever people live, they produce garbage. Most of our everyday garbage is taken to landfills, where it is burned or buried.

There are no landfills in the sky, and millions of pieces of garbage now float in orbit around Earth. This garbage is called space junk. Most of these pieces are dust-sized specks of dirt that break off satellites. Some pieces are as big as baseballs. Some pieces are even larger!

Scientists at the Johnson Space Center keep track of all the space junk around Earth. They use computers to make pictures like this one. Each white dot represents a piece of space junk.

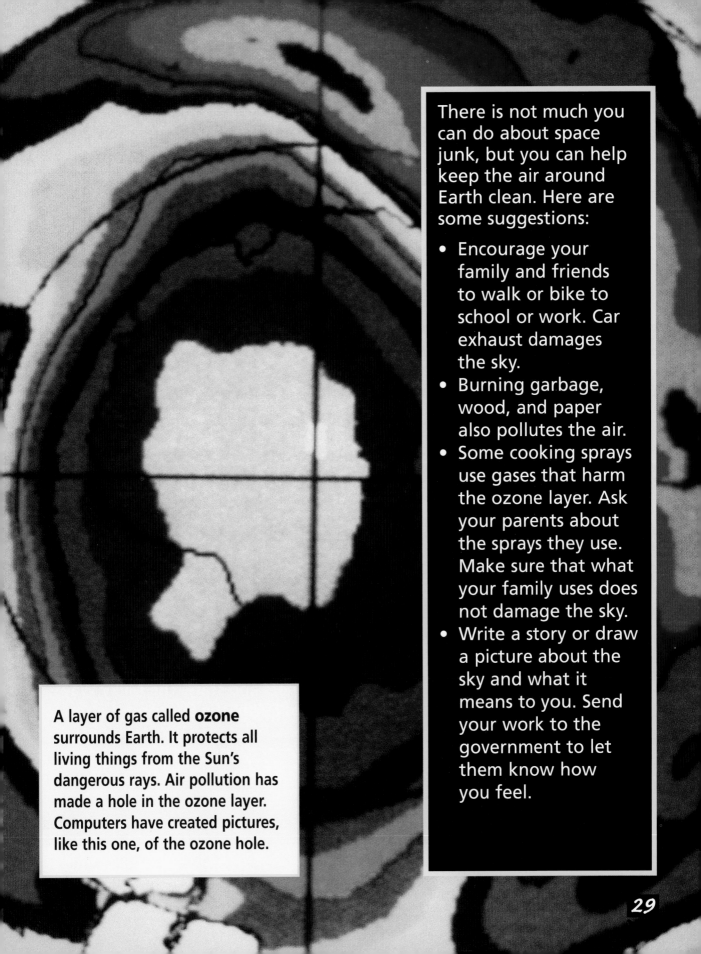

There is not much you can do about space junk, but you can help keep the air around Earth clean. Here are some suggestions:

- Encourage your family and friends to walk or bike to school or work. Car exhaust damages the sky.
- Burning garbage, wood, and paper also pollutes the air.
- Some cooking sprays use gases that harm the ozone layer. Ask your parents about the sprays they use. Make sure that what your family uses does not damage the sky.
- Write a story or draw a picture about the sky and what it means to you. Send your work to the government to let them know how you feel.

A layer of gas called **ozone** surrounds Earth. It protects all living things from the Sun's dangerous rays. Air pollution has made a hole in the ozone layer. Computers have created pictures, like this one, of the ozone hole.

Other Sky Facts

The sky is a big place. Here are a few more facts that may answer some of your questions about the sky.

We see blue skies
because of light and air.
Sunlight is a mixture of all the colors in the rainbow. When sunlight passes through ice and water droplets in the air, the colors in the light separate. Each of the colors is scattered across the sky. The blue and violet lights scatter the most. They spread so widely across the sky that it seems blue.

You can see
the Milky Way from Earth.
Earth is part of a galaxy called the Milky Way. A galaxy is a collection of planets and stars. The Milky Way includes Earth, the Sun, and the rest of our Solar System. On clear nights, you can see it with the naked eye. It looks like a fuzzy streak across the sky.

Stars twinkle and flicker

because we are looking at them through the atmosphere. Light from the stars travels toward Earth. It is bent over and over again by particles and gases. This bending creates the twinkling effect you see.

Supernovas

are stars that have exploded and become brighter than the Sun. A supernova can outshine an entire galaxy before it fades away.

The Moon is blue

on very rare occasions. Some months have two full moons. When this happens, the second moon is called a blue moon.

Glossary

atmosphere: the layers of gases around Earth.

comets: huge balls of ice, rock, and frozen gases.

energy: the ability to make things move or change.

force: a push or a pull.

helium: a colorless, odorless gas.

hydrogen: a colorless, odorless gas.

meteors: rocks that fall into Earth's atmosphere.

nebulas: clouds of dust and gases in space.

northern lights: the streamers and bands of light that appear in the northern sky at night.

orbit (v): to follow a curved path around an object.

oxygen: a colorless, odorless gas.

ozone: a form of oxygen that protects Earth from ultraviolet energy.

reflect: to bend or fold back, or cause to change direction.

Solar System: the Sun and everything that orbits around it.

sundogs: small halos near the Sun.

telescope: a device that makes faraway objects look closer.

water vapor: water that is in the form of a gas.

Index

Web Sites

www.dustbunny.com/afk/sky/sky.htm

www.wfu.edu/albatross/kids_sats.htm

kidsastronomy.tqn.com/msub1.htm

www.azstarnet.com/anubis/zaphome.htm

Some web sites stay current longer than others. For further web sites, use your search engines to locate the following topics: *aircraft, meteorology, ozone, satellites,* and *supernova.*